the secret of
a powerful inner life

Other books by Graham Cooke

Crafted Prayer
The Language of Love
Developing Your Prophetic Gifting
A Divine Confrontation

the secret of
a powerful inner life

Developing Genuine Spirituality

being with God series

Graham Cooke

Chosen
Grand Rapids, Michigan

Published by Chosen Books
A division of Baker Publishing Group
P.O. Box 6287, Grand Rapids, MI 49516-6287
www.chosenbooks.com

Printed in the United States of America

Originally published under the title *Towards a Powerful Inner Life*
by Sovereign World Limited of Tonbridge, Kent, England

       Library of Congress Cataloging-in-Publication Data
Cooke, Graham.
   [Toward a powerful inner life]
   The secret of a powerful inner life : developing genuine
spirituality / Graham Cooke.
      p. cm. – (Being with God)
   Originally published: Toward a powerful inner life. Tonbridge,
Kent, England : Sovereign World Ltd., 2003.
   ISBN 0-8007-9382-X (pbk.)
   1. Spiritual life–Christianity. I. Title.

BV4501.3.C664 2004
248.4–dc22

                            2004050019

I dedicate this book to the members of Odyssey, the businessmen's spirituality group in California that I colead with my great friend Tim Dickerson.

Our times together have been a compelling mixture of grace, search for truth, impacting dialogue, friendship, laughter and good wine. Thanks!

contents

introduction

It is a statement we find easy to believe on our good
days and nearly impossible to fathom on our bad
ones—God has a dream for our lives. He has a plan
and a goal for each of us that will be realized. God is
doing something, and everything is going to be all
right. It is a deep work—one that will hold us steady
during our darkest days, when everything and
everyone is against us. Once we accept that God is
constantly and consistently working in our lives, we
can be at peace.

As our lives unfold, God touches area after area,
bringing every part under His rule. What is He working
on in you right now? "Everything," we quip easily.
God, however, focuses on something more particular
than "everything."

Perhaps He is touching your emotions. It is easy to
allow our emotions to run the show, and God wants to
touch that. For others, it is our analytical mind-set that
wants to understand everything logically before we
commit ourselves to trusting the Lord. Some people are
not in the habit of activating their wills or have failed

to see that the will is the prime vehicle for cooperating with the Holy Spirit. Our souls—the emotions, mind and will—can be a hurdle to an experience with God.

Whatever God is touching in you is what He wants to bring under His rule. He wants to work on certain parts of you, but it does not have to be a painful process. The pain depends on how you approach the task. One of my mentors once told me, "Graham, die quietly. No one wants to hear you scream." God's touch can be a gentle caress if we will lay down our wills and agendas and let Him work.

We can approach God's work in our lives in two ways—we can try to do it for Him, or we can allow Him to do it for us. The apostle Paul wrote, "Likewise you also, reckon yourselves to be dead indeed to sin, but alive to God in Christ Jesus our Lord" (Romans 6:11). We can live under the idea that we need to die to everything, but that still puts the focus on ourselves and our wills.

> "The thief does not come except to steal, and to kill, and to destroy. I have come that they may have life, and that they may have it more abundantly."
> —Jesus, John 10:10

The second part of the verse, "but alive to God in Christ Jesus our Lord," takes that same change in behavior and attitude and allows God to perform it. Rather than kill ourselves, we can let God live in the area that needs God's touch.

What a choice! Our very happiness depends on how we respond to God's touch. Will we kill ourselves or let

God come alive? Our religious ability is so subtle in this. How can it be God's refinement if we do not feel intense pain? Without even realizing it, we have taken over the Holy Spirit's job of bringing ourselves under God's rule: "*I'll* do it," we say. Our soul takes the issue, sticks it in the oven for a while and waits until God is looking away to pull it back out again. Trying to die to it makes us preoccupied with what we are not. But living in Christ Jesus makes us preoccupied with Him. We become alive to God, which automatically makes us dead to ourselves.

Allowing God to live in us and make the changes necessary for His dream for us to come true can still be painful sometimes. The discomfort, however, is more than taken care of by God's grace and mercy for us.

As Christians, we must train our minds, emotions and wills to submit to our spirits. Our spirits will have to say no to our souls from time to time, and the soul will have to grin and bear it. We must be disciplined to take our thoughts captive:

► *No, I'm not thinking that—I'm thinking about purity and love and God's grace.*
► *No, I'm not thinking that—I'm thinking about how I can be generous for the Lord's sake.*
► *No, I'm not thinking that—I'm thinking about how I can show that person the love of God.*

> ▶ *No, I'm not thinking that—I'm thinking about how I can bless this pastor who has poured his heart into his little church.*
>
> ▶ *No, I'm not thinking that—I'm thinking about the peace I've found in Jesus.*

The same exercise must be done with our emotions, constantly bringing them back to the purity of God. Emotions are not wrong; they are, for the most part, healthy and releasing. But they are only a part of us and must not be allowed to dominate our lives. Emotions and thoughts are designed to enable us to focus on our Creator so that we may perceive people and events with His understanding.

The will is the vehicle whereby we check our feelings and perceptions with the Holy Spirit before acting on them. If our thought lives and emotions are more active than our wills, the tendency is for us to break down into our carnality and not be released into our God-given spirituality.

The Holy Spirit always offers us an alternative to our internal emotional predicament. He gives us comfort for grief, mercy instead of anger, grace rather than resentment, joy to overwhelm sadness, compassion to replace confusion and acceptance in our loneliness.

Paul loved the life of the spirit: "There is therefore now no condemnation to those who are in Christ Jesus, who do not walk according to the flesh, but according to the Spirit" (Romans 8:1). God knows the struggle we have, but He does not want to condemn us for it. If you mess up for a day, do not condemn yourself for it—God does not. There is always tomorrow, with fresh mercy.

Because I spend time on the road preaching, people always ask me how I slept the night before. Sometimes I sleep well, but most of the time I am asleep for an hour, awake for an hour, asleep for a couple more hours. There are many nights when I do not sleep at all. On those nights, I just smile and say, "I didn't sleep at all, but that's okay—I'll get another chance tonight."

Life in the spirit is a little bit like that. God does not beat us up over missing it one day. In fact, His love bubbles over for us: "I know the struggle you're having, but it's a good fight. I promise, it's a good fight you can win. Just stop condemning yourself for it. If we don't win today, we'll win tomorrow. Every day is a new day, by My mercy."

> "He sent His Son with power to save from guilt and darkness and the grave: Wonders of grace to God belong; repeat His mercies in your song."
> —Isaac Watts and John Hatton

The next morning we wake up, and God says, "Okay, it's a new day. I've gotten rid of yesterday; let's not carry anything forward into today. Let's have a fresh crack at it, together. I refuse to allow you to beat yourself up over what happened yesterday."

Paul's instructions should be at the forefront of our mind at all times:

There is therefore now no condemnation to those who are in Christ Jesus, who do not walk according to the flesh, but according to the Spirit. For the law of the Spirit of life in Christ Jesus has made me free from the law of sin and death. For what the law could not do in that it was weak through the flesh, God did by sending His own Son in the likeness of sinful flesh, on account of sin: He condemned sin in the flesh, that the righteous requirement of the law might be fulfilled in us who do not walk according to the flesh but according to the Spirit. For those who live according to the flesh set their minds on the things of the flesh, but those who live according to the Spirit, the things of the Spirit. For to be carnally minded is death, but to be spiritually minded is life and peace.

Romans 8:1–6

The New Living Translation of the Bible puts verse 6 even more clearly: "If your sinful nature controls your mind, there is death. But if the Holy Spirit controls your mind, there is life and peace." Our joy, every day, is to come to God anew, "having boldness to enter the Holiest by the blood of Jesus" (Hebrews 10:19). We are welcome to approach His throne. We can—and must—enter His presence every day, with confidence, to see His dreams unfold in our lives. This is our call and our privilege.

the secret of a powerful inner life

soul versus spirit

We are beings at war with ourselves. Inside each of us are two parts in conflict—a soul, otherwise known as the outer man, and a spirit, also known as the inner man. These two pieces of the whole strive for complete control of who we are. Each desperately wants to run the show, but only one can. The apostle Paul writes about the battle of these two halves, using the word *spiritual* to describe the inner man and the word *carnal* to describe the outer man:

> For we know that the law is spiritual, but I am carnal, sold under sin. For what I am doing, I do not understand. For what I will to do, that I do not practice; but what I hate, that I do. If, then, I do what I will not to do, I agree with the law that it is good. But now, it is no longer I who do it, but sin that dwells in me. For I know that in me (that is, in my flesh) nothing good

dwells; for to will is present with me, but how to
perform what is good I do not find. For the good that I
will to do, I do not do; but the evil I will not to do, that
I practice. Now if I do what I will not to do, it is no
longer I who do it, but sin that dwells in me. I find then
a law, that evil is present with me, the one who wills to
do good. For I delight in the law of God according to
the inward man. But I see another law in my members,
warring against the law of my mind, and bringing me
into captivity to the law of sin which is in my members.
O wretched man that I am! Who will deliver me from
this body of death? I thank God—through Jesus Christ
our Lord! So then, with the mind I myself serve the law
of God, but with the flesh the law of sin.

Romans 7:14-25

God has called us to be ruled by our spirits, to submit
the outer man (our souls) to that inner man. As Paul
writes, we must begin "warring" against ourselves,
subjecting our souls (our minds, emotions and wills) to
our spirits (that part of us that connects with God).
Before we were Christians, we did what we wanted, we
went where we pleased, we ruled our own life. But with
salvation came a call from a different king—our souls
must bow their knees to the reign of God.

This can be quite a battle. The spirit, which hears the
whisper of God, exerts pressure on the soulish will to
change its behavior. The soul, conversely, is more in
love with the *idea* of God than with God *Himself.* The

soul drags its heels, trying desperately to avoid surrendering to the spirit. It manifests itself in willful displays, deluded thinking and odd emotional behavior. The soul refuses to surrender easily to the spirit, because the soul wants to be number one. It will rule us to the point of ruining us. For example, the soul believes in self-gratification—it resists God. The spirit, on the other hand, knows the power and satisfaction of God.

Our souls do not, because of our finiteness, understand the ways of God. They cannot fathom why He does what He does. Our minds are just too limited by time and space to see the richness of the Lord's activities. When we find ourselves in trouble, our souls know what they want from God: *Get me out of here! Lift me up out of this mess!* The soul tries its best to avoid entering the process of submitting to the spirit.

> "To be taken with love for a soul, God does not look upon its greatness, but the greatness of its humility."
> —St. John of the Cross

Souls hate being weak—they would much rather flex their intellectual, willful or emotional muscles to prove their strength. Our souls do not want to surrender control, because it seems illogical to do so.

Yet soul power must be broken, or we cannot serve God effectively. Our souls need to recognize that they will be truly happy only when we have no authority but have taken the attitude of serving what God has placed within us—our spirits. The soul will only find peace and fulfillment and full expression when it is a vehicle for the spirit to operate.

Left unconquered, the soul keeps us open and vulnerable to external pressures and attacks. Learning how to live in the spirit gives us the opportunity, because of our devotion and submission to God, to reverse all the activity of the enemy and render his schemes useless. With the soul in control, the enemy is free to buffet us and leave us in the grip of the very pain we were called to put on him. If we can learn to submit our outer man to our inner man, nothing from the outside world will be able to shake who we are in Christ.

The story of the sisters Mary and Martha found in Luke 10:38–42 is a perfect example of one person living under the power of her soul and of the other living under the power of her spirit. Mary, whose spirit was drawn and electrified by the Spirit of God, sat at Jesus's feet and listened as He spoke and taught. "Mary has chosen that good part, which will not be taken away from her," Jesus said (verse 42). Martha, on the other hand, had too many preparations on her mind and fell into an emotional outburst to try to get Mary to serve her agenda. "Martha, Martha, you are worried and troubled about many things," Jesus said. "But one thing is needed" (verses 41–42). The issue here is primacy. Martha's concerns were, in fact, legitimate. But in the context of placing soul under spirit, she had made *doing* more important than *being*. When that happens, we are not living from the inside out but from the opposite dimension. We must place real value on the presence of God above all other concerns, no matter how pressing.

There are times when we have to work and times when we have to rest—the book of Ecclesiastes makes that clear. We do not always get to sit at the feet of Jesus and do nothing. This story, however, is an illustration of what we have promoted, when push comes to shove. Does the presence of God have primacy in our lives? Have we allowed our spirits to sit at the feet of Jesus? Or are we constantly thinking about our temporal concerns? It seems paradoxical, but if we can learn to rest at Jesus's feet, we will find we can do the temporal things properly.

> "How happy I am to see myself imperfect and be in need of God's mercy."
> —St. Thérèse of the Child Jesus and the Holy Face

When we live in our spirits, we do not need reassurance. We have a built-in testimony—the Holy Spirit bears witness with our spirits that we are the children of God.

the three-part person

According to Scripture, every man and woman who has ever lived has three parts, a soul, a spirit and a body. Paul wrote, "Now may the God of peace Himself sanctify you completely; and may your whole spirit, soul, and body be preserved blameless at the coming of our Lord Jesus Christ" (1 Thessalonians 5:23). The body and soul often conspire and work together against the spirit. In God's design, however, He intended the Holy Spirit to dwell in and mingle with our spirits. That spiritual man would then govern the soul, which is made up of mind, emotions and will.

To live happily and successfully with God, we must become vehicles of the spirit. Our bodies will be used as the outward expression of whatever is in command— our souls or our spirits. To be our fullest expression in Christ, our souls must understand that they cannot, and must not, act on their own volition. The spirit man, according to the relationship it has with the Holy Spirit, must give the soul instruction and authority. The soul has to be won, mastered and ruled by the spirit if we want to know the higher ways of God. Our souls need to be saved every day.

The Bible has many verses explaining the need for the soul to submit to the spirit:

▶ "For I delight in the law of God according to the inward man" (Romans 7:22).
▶ "That He would grant you, according to the riches of His glory, to be strengthened with might through His Spirit in the inner man, that Christ may dwell in your hearts through faith" (Ephesians 3:16–17).

► "But you are not in the flesh but in the Spirit, if indeed the Spirit of God dwells in you. Now if anyone does not have the Spirit of Christ, he is not His" (Romans 8:9).

► "Therefore we do not lose heart. Even though our outward man is perishing, yet the inward man is being renewed day by day" (2 Corinthians 4:16).

When the Bible talks about the innermost being, it is referring to the spirit. When it talks about the outer man, it is referring to the soul and body. God lives in the human spirit; His Holy Spirit mingles with our spirits.

> "The inner man, the spirit, wears the outer man, the soul and body."

The concept of inner and outer beings can be likened to clothing. The inner man, the spirit, wears the outer man, the soul and body. To be effective for Christ, we must release the inner man. To be fulfilled and joyful, the spirit must govern the soul.

what is the spirit?

The spirit is only ever subject to, and in the presence of, God. It is the part of us that is eternal. It constantly communes with God Himself, only having dealings with Him. To interact with the physical world, it must operate through the soul and body. The spirit is the part of us that finds its refuge in God. When the psalmist sings, "He is my refuge and my fortress; My God, in Him I will trust" (Psalm 91:2), he refers to his spirit finding safety within God's presence. It is a place inside us that cannot be touched by anything out in the world because it lives in the presence of God.

The Father has several wonderfully visual images of what life in the spirit looks like. He is our refuge, fortress, high tower and hiding place; we nestle under the shadow of His wings. One of the prime goals of our relationships with God must be to learn to access these safe places daily. We need to learn the business of stepping back into the internal provision of God in the spirit. Do we take refuge in Him when under pressure and attack? Do we wait patiently to discern His heart before committing ourselves to an action? This is the loving discipline of the spirit that takes the control away from our souls so that we can respond to God and not react to events.

When the enemy comes calling, we shouldn't rush out to meet him in battle. Instead, we should retreat into our spirits first, entering the presence of God. When we are there, God can give us intelligence, resources and strategies to destroy the enemy. In leadership, the first difficulties we face are not the work of the ministry or other people—but ourselves. We are our own worst enemies, because we refuse to subject our souls to our spirits. If we allow our spirits to govern the way we act and lead, we will have God's empowerment to carry on.

weakness of the soul

Our souls are not our enemies. If we have committed our lives to Jesus, the soul loves God, but unfortunately it is like an immature adolescent that lives in our skin— our souls want to meet God on our own terms. *I want God to do things for me, but I want to run my own life,* the soul moans. *I want to live how I like to live.* Our souls want to relegate God to a basic insurance policy— if I need a bit of help, He's there. Otherwise, He's locked away in the safety deposit box.

The soul was designed to serve, a statement that raises the question, "But if it's not serving God, who is it serving?" Our souls will serve us and will even serve the enemy. They fight to stay in control. Religious activity provides a set of external rules that our souls strive to keep so they can maintain control of their destinies. Much of the Pharisaical activity recorded in Scripture was soulish and manipulative, concerned more with retaining power than demonstrating servanthood, more aware of status than humility and more open to controlling with power than fathering and mentoring. We are all Pharisees, being healed.

> "It is sweet to think of Jesus; but it is sweeter to do His will."
> —Blessed Mary of Jesus Crucified

Until the time of salvation, our souls ruled unopposed through our minds, wills and emotions. Our spirits were dead, with no concept of God. Before

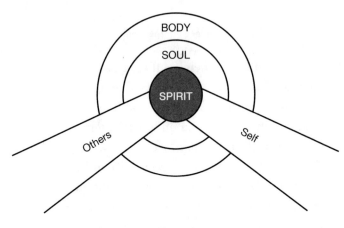

Figure 1

salvation, we lived as we pleased. We were dominated by soulishness and self-interest (see Figure 1).

God breaks into our lives at salvation, causing a massive battle within ourselves. The spirit is boosted and begins to push the soul to express love for God, ourselves and other people. The soul hates this, for it is no longer in full control. We are born again, and our spirit is revitalized. The soul must submit to that spirit man, or it will suffer one of two fates—it either becomes carnal or flesh.

Flesh is the sinful appetite of the *body*, anything we do for self-gratification—sex, drugs, overeating and so on. *Carnality* is the sinful appetite of the *soul*, or what happens when we run our lives through the soul and not the spirit. Although we may want to live for God, our carnality refuses to relinquish control to Him. We

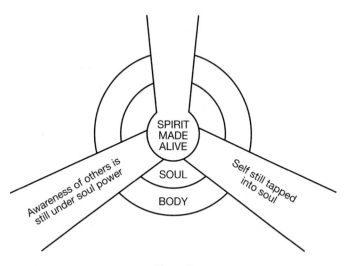

Figure 2

become religious and Pharisaical, living to please ourselves but calling it godliness.

When we are born again, our spirit is revitalized (see Figure 2). Now the battle for supremacy begins. We come under the conflict of two natures, as detailed in Romans 7:14–25. Salvation brings another measure of rule to our lives. Soul power has to be broken or we cannot serve God effectively.

an ancient conflict

This epic battle of soul versus spirit is not a recent development. Modern humanity is in good company with every generation that has walked the earth since

God created humankind. When Adam and Eve ate the bad fruit in the Garden of Eden, they were immediately changed—their souls became the rulers of their lives. The couple had access to God's wisdom through the spirit, but the enemy convinced them there was more than that available to them. The temptation in Eden centered on the issue of wisdom:

> Now the serpent was more cunning than any beast of the field which the LORD God had made. And he said to the woman, "Has God indeed said, 'You shall not eat of every tree of the garden'?"
>
> And the woman said to the serpent, "We may eat the fruit of the trees of the garden; but of the fruit of the tree which is in the midst of the garden, God has said, 'You shall not eat it, nor shall you touch it, lest you die.'"
>
> Then the serpent said to the woman, "You will not surely die. For God knows that in the day you eat of it your eyes will be opened, and you will be like God, knowing good and evil."
>
> Genesis 3:1–5

Satan's advice to humans was to reach across the boundaries set by God and seize the resources of wisdom for themselves. "You will be like God," he said. The serpent conned them into believing there could be a life without dependence on God. "Depend on yourself," he essentially lied, "and when you get into a really sticky situation, then call on God. In the meantime, go with what your soul tells you." This is a lie every man and woman has struggled with since.

Israel's history is littered with examples of the nation turning its back on God and finding itself in terrible situations. "Everyone did what was right in his own eyes," as the book of Judges puts it many times. In those moments of rebellion, a famine or invading kingdom strikes; the Israelites, in fear and disarray, repent and beg God to save them. In His mercy, the Lord heals the situation, delivering the unfaithful nation. For a while, the people again serve Him before drifting back into their old pattern of doing what seems right to their own minds, emotions and wills.

Satan lied, of course—there was no wisdom in the Tree of the Knowledge of Good and Evil. In fact, God's wisdom was contained in the Tree of Life. The tree of good and evil brought only death, and humans were driven out of the Garden of Eden. But God would raise up a Redeemer who would come and open the door for humans to return to Him. In the meantime, however, fallen men and women strove to live by their own wisdom, motivated by selfish ambition and jealousy.

We see this pattern especially clearly in the field of philosophy. What is philosophy but human wisdom? It is mostly about how some person thinks about something. I often visit the philosophical section when I am in a bookstore to find out what people are thinking about now. If you let your spirit do the looking through those books and thoughts, you'll come to a startling realization—rarely does philosophy take us into the presence of God and make us conscious of Him. Rather, it appeals to our minds, helping us explain something of our state of being, but adding nothing to our standing in Christ. It can give credence to our souls but may contribute nothing to our spirits. It is empty and potentially deceptive, like a cloud without rain. Philosophy sounds great, but it does not actually mean anything. It does not connect with our spirits; it just makes us more self-absorbed. Intellectual people often struggle with a similar issue—they live so much in their minds that they have no spiritual perception whatsoever. When you talk to people whose intellect is their god, they will try to defeat you with logic and science. It is frustrating—you want to have a spiritual conversation, but they want to have a soulish one.

> "Intellectual people often struggle with a similar issue—they live so much in their minds that they have no spiritual perception whatsoever."

Philosophy is but one example of how humans devise means to attain their own goals, falling prey to a wisdom that is earthly, unspiritual and ultimately demonic:

> This wisdom does not descend from above, but is earthly, sensual, demonic. For where envy and self-seeking

exist, confusion and every evil thing are there. But the
wisdom that is from above is first pure, then peaceable,
gentle, willing to yield, full of mercy and good fruits,
without partiality and without hypocrisy. Now the
fruit of righteousness is sown in peace by those who
make peace.

James 3:15–18

When we hear wisdom, we feel good about ourselves.
It touches our hearts and helps us to see God in a better
light. That fresh light gives us a better view of
ourselves as well. It touches how we feel about who we
are. Yet when humans ate the fruit from the Tree of the
Knowledge of Good and Evil, the spirit was dethroned.
Divine order in fallen humanity was lost. Our spirits
were cut off from God, and we lost our God-given
authority and power. Adam and Eve became more
aware of their own nakedness—what they were not and
did not possess—than the provision and covering of the
Father's love. God's love first clothed them in
righteousness, but then they sought to cover themselves
at the expense of their relationship with the Father.

Adam, Eve and all of their descendants now had to
fill that void of power and authority in their lives. The
soul swelled up and took the lead. Our soul's power—
what makes our minds, wills and emotions happy—
and our physical appetites became the driving force
behind our lives.

the disciples' battle

Another example of the battle of soul versus spirit can be found in the lives of Jesus's disciples. In Mark 4 we read that Jesus, the greatest weatherman of all time, saw a storm brewing on the Sea of Galilee and made a suggestion: "Let's go for a boat ride." He and His disciples piled into the boat and set sail. A few minutes later, Jesus was asleep in the back.

Many of Jesus's friends were experienced fishermen, but they had never before met a storm like this—a storm engineered by God for a particular purpose. Things were bad, the waves were fierce and Jesus was asleep. How could He have been so tranquil? How could He have slept through this? What was wrong with Him?

I have seen many times that when you put a spiritual person in a room with a soulish person and subject them both to the same experience, the soulish person will accuse the spiritual of not caring. Why? Because a spiritual person is peaceful. How can the other person care, the soulish reasons, if that person is not showing anxiety? We have made anxiety a virtue. Actually, the spiritual person does care, but cares from a different place. Soulish people wear worry in their minds, emotions and wills, while spiritual people wear theirs in the presence of God. The lesson is that anxiety will never overcome anything.

"Peace, be still."
—Jesus, Mark 4:39

When we learn to live in the realm of the spirit, people think we do not care about things. "Teacher, do You not care that we are perishing?" the disciples asked Jesus (Mark 4:38). Of course He did. He just stood up and did the thing they should have done—He spoke to what was happening in the physical world from what was happening in His spirit.

the cancer of the soul

Our souls will be a hindrance if we do not bring them under the rule and authority of our spirits. I became a Christian on my nineteenth birthday. For nineteen years, my human spirit had been dead to God. Although alive and functioning—the spirit of unregenerate people does not cease to exist—it had been "dead in trespasses and sins" (Ephesians 2:1).

Life and death in Scripture always centers on relationship. *Life* means a person is rightly related to God who is the source of all life. *Death* means a person is cut off from God through sin.

The human spirit in its unregenerate state is still able to connect with the spiritual realm but can only reach and touch the dark side where death reigns. This is the occult realm, which may appear benign and attractive but contains evil seductive spirits who can suck us into their terrifying control. For this reason Scripture prohibits spiritualism, divination and fortunetelling, as

they lead vulnerable people into potential and actual
enslavement.

Until I became a Christian, my soul and my body
governed every aspect of my life—I did whatever
pleased me. Then one day the light of God shone into
me. Everything changed! From that moment on, I have
been at odds with myself, working to make my soul
submit to my spirit. Before salvation, the spirit is dead,
unconnected to God. When Jesus came in, He changed
all that, plugging my spirit into His—I was truly alive.

I used to make my own decisions, reigning and
ruling through my soul. My mind, emotions and will
dominated through my body. I was self-centered, self-
referential and cold, offering only conditional love.
What can I get out of this relationship? I used to think.
What's in it for me? When I lived in my body and soul,
I was always subject to external influences.

Before we are saved, we are buffeted by the enemy in
so many ways. Some soulish men and women
understand the will in an occult way, using it to
dominate other people and to lead them away from
God. They use systems and philosophies like New Age
to take people on a quest far from the Lord. All the will
wants is power over other people. Most who go into
witchcraft and the occult are in it for pride, power,
money and sex. They want to dominate people.
Witchcraft is a suffocating force, which is why we must
get rid of it in the Church.

Other soulish people are at the mercy of their emotions. Everything is about feelings. "I feel this," they say. A lot of counseling has too much to do with emotions, which makes what we are feeling at any given moment the central thing in our lives. We are told to release our inner selves and that our emotions and what we feel is all-important.

> "It is not so essential to think much as to love much."
> —St. Teresa of Jesus

Others are dominated by bodily appetites and physical drives. It could be sex, food, fitness and so on. We go to a gym and find ourselves surrounded by body Nazis—all looking at our puny shapes and shaking their heads in disdain. They are there hours and hours, day after day. Some people are dominated by how they look. Perhaps they need an extra room to hold all their clothes. Possessions and images hold other people.

There is nothing wrong with looking good or owning something, unless it dominates our lives. We can be well dressed, own a beautiful house and drive a nice car, but we must not allow those things to dominate us. The result of serving these other items is ruinous. Our souls and bodies were not meant to rule us. They are incapable of guiding us. When we are materialistic, there is a power struggle between all of our competing desires, all clamoring to be satisfied, all claiming to be of paramount importance.

In such a state we end up hopelessly at war with

ourselves—divided, imbalanced and a slave to sin. We see this phenomenon in the Corinthian church. These people had become Christians but did not understand that the spirit needed to rule the soul. Paul, as an apostle, had to correct their carnality. He identified their sexual sin, which was horrific—one churchgoer was even having sex with his mother or stepmother (see 1 Corinthians 5:1). Their souls ran the show in Corinth, and Paul had to step in and right the ship:

> For I indeed, as absent in body but present in spirit, have already judged (as though I were present) him who has so done this deed. In the name of our Lord Jesus Christ, when you are gathered together, along with my spirit, with the power of our Lord Jesus Christ, deliver such a one to Satan for the destruction of the flesh, that his spirit may be saved in the day of the Lord Jesus.
>
> 1 Corinthians 5:3–5

Paul knew in his spirit what was happening in Corinth and, as an apostle, brought correction. His desire was to protect the spiritual men and women of Corinth from soulish self-gratification.

the unregenerate man

It is essential that we understand what we have been called out of. The unregenerate person, who lives according to the soul, not the spirit, is wide open to the power of the demonic. Such a person's spirit, while dead to the things of God, is alive to the touch of the enemy—when people become involved in occult things, evil power can be transferred into their spirits. The spirit has lost its link with God, the source of life, and has become no better than the rest of human fallen nature.

The human spirit is created to connect to an external source of power or authority. Therefore, the unregenerate person's spirit has fallen under the power of Satan and is dead to God, as Paul writes to the Christians in Ephesus:

> And you He made alive, who were dead in trespasses and sins, in which you once walked according to the course of this world, according to the prince of the power of the air, the spirit who now works in the sons of disobedience, among whom also we all once conducted ourselves in the lusts of our flesh, fulfilling the desires of the flesh and of the mind, and were by nature children of wrath, just as the others.
>
> Ephesians 2:1–3

Paul was writing about a spirit under the power of evil. If you travel to minister in certain parts of the world, you cannot simply go in and preach the Gospel. First, the Lord must do signs and wonders to deliver people of evil spirits. They have to be set free to hear the Good News. Only then can they be saved.

I have experienced this in my own ministry throughout the developing world, where a Christian has to go head-to-head with a witch doctor or some other powerful occult practitioner. Ministry in those places is about continual confrontation with the powers of darkness. The battle is often physical and the demonic is visible and intimidating. "Normal" ministry methods are overturned when dealing with the occult. Living in the spirit is essential or one cannot compete with the works of darkness. To be successful in sharing the Gospel, we must know exactly who we are and what we have to overcome. These people's spirits, so choked by the demonic, understand only power. Our word means nothing out there. What they want to know is, "Is your God stronger than mine?" And if He is, they will follow Him.

In the West, the demonic force is much subtler, rooted in unreality and fantasy. It manifests itself in the headlong pursuit of relentless self-gratification. Millions of people are financially in debt in the chase for self-worth and the feel-good factor. Emotional healing is big business in the West. Mental illness is a modern-day plague with suicides among all generations at an all-time high. It is the spirit of the age, and the Western Church, in particular, is influenced by it. Soulish Christianity is rampant in the West in a Church driven almost universally by consumerism. "My needs, my rights, my desires" dominate the thinking of

Western believers who pick and choose the church program most able to fulfill their requirements. There is little thought of service, sacrifice or meeting the needs of others. It is little wonder that the occult religions have taken hold in the West—it is easy to outwit a complacent Church. Soulish Christianity is a pushover for the forces of darkness. The enemy wins every battle with ease because most Christians fail to show up for the fight.

We must ask ourselves some important questions:

▶ When was the last time I successfully encountered the enemy?
▶ How many times have I gone through difficult circumstances and failed to notice the power behind the situation?
▶ When was the last time I took specific thoughts captive or controlled my emotions by faith?

Now reflect on these issues. Is the inability to rule in our own lives directly linked to our ineffectiveness in spiritual warfare? While Jesus said, "The ruler of this world is coming, and he has nothing in Me" (John 14:30), Paul expressed it this way: "[Give no] place to the devil" (Ephesians 4:27).

Christians are never weak numerically. One person, with God, is always in the majority. But we are weak when we do not understand who we are in God or what

He has provided for us. That is why the Church is so atrophied in many parts of the world. People die spiritually every day trying to reach the lost in these occult-laced places. There is a demonic power out there that is very real, which is why it is vital for us to get God's power flowing in our lives.

"One person, with God, is always in the majority."

Unregenerate men and women can contact the spiritual realm—their spirits are functional, but dead to God. If a spirit cannot connect with God, it will connect with something, anything, else. If it will not reach for the third heaven, where God dwells, it will settle for contact with the second heaven, home of Satan and his demons.

I have met occult people who move in genuine power. They can prophesy incredibly accurately. This is nothing new; Acts 16 could have told us that. A slave girl, possessed by a spirit of divination, had followed Paul and Silas around for days, prophesying, "These men are the servants of the Most High God, who proclaim to us the way of salvation" (verse 17). That prophetic word is completely accurate. More than that, it is almost worshipful: "The Most High God." Yet her words were not from the Spirit of God. Scripture tells us Paul was grieved in his spirit by the girl's plight, so he turned to her and said to the demon, "I command you in the name of Jesus Christ to come out of her" (verse 18), and it did.

Humanity in its unregenerate state can have a
relationship with spiritual beings who are not of God.
Human spirits will reach into the realm
of death and darkness for that
connection, which explains the
proliferation of spiritism, New Age,
occultism, tarot cards and pagan
religions. These all lead to death. Behind
these activities is a demonic presence
looking to suck the human spirit dry. Solomon wrote:

> "I surrendered unto Him all
> there was of me, everything!
> Then for the first time, I
> realized what it meant to
> have real power."
> —Kathryn Kuhlman

> There is a way that seems right to a man,
> But its end is the way of death.
>
> Proverbs 14:12

spirit life

A spirit in relationship with God experiences such
abundant life that it is almost difficult to describe.
When our spirits have submitted to God and begun to
take control of our souls, amazing fruit is produced. We
love others more because we ourselves are fully
immersed and settled in God's love.

We have been made in the image and likeness of
God. Our spirits were intended by Him to relate us with
God, enabling us to receive wisdom and life from Him.
Relationship with God is what the Bible calls "life." So
to be rightly related with God is life, and to be cut off

from Him is death. We still exist, laughing, crying and working, but are spiritually dead because we have no communion with God, the source of life.

We are always welcome in God's presence, because we live like a much-loved child. Our purpose is to love God. When our spirits are alive, our minds can have life and peace. Life flows out of our spirits and into our mortal bodies. As Paul writes, "For if by the one man's offense death reigned through the one, much more those who receive abundance of grace and of the gift of righteousness will reign in life through the One, Jesus Christ" (Romans 5:17). The pathway to a glorious life is determined by how we yield ourselves to God.

> "The pathway to a glorious life is determined by how we yield ourselves to God."

We can come boldly into God's presence when we are alive in the spirit. When my wife, Heather, was pregnant with our second child, God told me he was going to be a boy and he would make me laugh all the days of my life. "He's going to make you smile, Grae," God said. "He's going to teach you to be a son before Me."

God was right. Seth was a character from the beginning. Halfway out during the delivery, Seth wailed and smiled. I laughed—it was as if he were introducing himself: "Ta da! Get ready, folks!" He has been exactly what God told me he was destined to be. I have learned so much of how to be a son before a father by watching Seth. He is exuberant, ready and confident: "Tomorrow is another day!" Seth's life makes me smile. The Lord wants us to be like that with Him. Be ready for every new day. Enjoy His grace that is new every morning. Today, together, we are going to whip the world. And if we do not, there is always tomorrow.

Moreover, God develops our faith to rule over our feelings. Faith is cold-blooded and has no emotion attached to it. We can believe something even if we do not feel it. Many of us have become prisoners to our emotions, allowing them to run the show. God wants to put that back into its proper order. Feelings are like the tail end of a dog; they will just go along with whatever is in control. Emotions, in God's order, serve us and aid us in being with Him, people and ourselves.

Also, God uses His unconditional love to kill religiosity. The religious part of us has to be shocked by the nature of God. How can He love somebody that much? Does God love Saddam Hussein as much as He loves you? Does He love Osama bin Laden as much as He loves you? Absolutely. God loves those men. "But they're monsters!" our religiosity objects. Still, God loves them. I am not defending them or their actions, but God does love them. His love is shocking in that regard.

A true spirituality, not a soulish one, is cultivated by God. We see the difference between the two in how we pray. When the soul prays for strength, it always has itself as the focus: "Father, *I* pray that You will strengthen *me* by Your spirit, enabling *me* to stand and overcome *my* weakness so that *I* can fight and break through *my* circumstances." That prayer is packed full of references to I, me and my—the soul wants to receive power for itself.

> "We had a mighty downpouring of the Holy Spirit last Saturday night. This was preceded by the correcting of the people's view of true worship: Number one, to give unto God, not to receive. Number two, to please God, not to please ourselves."
> —Evan Roberts

When a spirit-led man or woman prays, he or she asks God to do whatever He wants to do: "Father, thank You that in my weakness You are strength. I submit to Your rule. Come and be my strength—live in me, and overcome me with Your power. Inhabit these circumstances, and glorify Your name in all You achieve." This prayer is completely different from the soulish.

God is breaking our self-preoccupation. I, me and myself—that era is ending. He is making us considerate, open-hearted and generous through the work of His cross. We must enjoy our weakness, because God flows through that weakness.

The Holy Spirit has an agenda for us—He wants us to come under His influence as He reveals and forms Christ in us. Jesus and the Holy Spirit are conspiring together for the glory of God.

Paul wrote, "If then you were raised with Christ, seek those things which are above, where Christ is, sitting at the right hand of God. Set your mind on things above, not on things on the earth. For you died, and your life is hidden with Christ in God" (Colossians 3:1-3). Our goal is to seek the things above both us and the enemy.

There are three levels of spirituality that we need to understand. The first level, the "first heaven," is the natural realm in which we live all the time. The second level, the "second heaven," is the realm where the demonic resides. The third and highest level, the "third heaven," is where God lives. Paul wrote, "But God, who is rich in mercy, because of His great love with which He loved us, even when we were dead in trespasses, made us alive together with Christ (by grace you have been saved), and raised us up together, and made us sit together in the heavenly places in Christ Jesus" (Ephesians 2:4-6).

The second level is where we do battle with the enemy, but the third level is where we are supposed to live. The tragedy for most Christians is that they are earthbound, stuck on the first level, in their spirituality. They are so dominated by fear, logic and reason that they can look only for physical evidence. But when we look for the evidence of God, we go above the first and second levels, above the principalities and powers, and dwell with Him.

Our goal must be to seek things not just above us, but above the enemy. Search out the third heaven, where God lives. We get a perspective of God in the third level that we cannot get on the ground. It is the difference between being an eagle and a turkey. We must set our mind on Christ above, not on the things of the earth.

"We get a perspective of God in the third level that we cannot get on the ground."

The key is to hide our lives with Christ in God. A spirit-led life is wrapped up in Jesus and protected by that refuge. If you are in Christ, He guards you. In the face of difficulty, we must step back into our spirit man and let Jesus protect us. Otherwise, the soul will try to do it for us, and that initiative is doomed to failure.

When we are attacked, we must not react. Instead, we should respond to God. Do not look at the circumstances—look at God. Step back into the spirit. Sometimes, the best thing to do is say nothing and let people unload all over you. Then ignore the temptation to lash back, and instead step into your spirit and the comfort of Christ. If you try to give out like for like, you are going to get hurt; but if you step back into your spirit, you are going to get healed.

God wants to bring us into a higher level of spirituality. Our spirit and His Spirit will mingle as we set our minds on the things above—having our souls submit to our spirits. God is intentional about everything in our lives. Knowing that, we can go into every situation and know that it is about our souls submitting to His will, as communicated to our spirits. In conflict, our prayers should be simple:

- ► *Lord, I want to give in to You right now.*
- ► *Lord, I quit. Please take over.*
- ► *Lord, teach me Your ways.*
- ► *Lord, show me Your path.*
- ► *Lord, show me what to do.*

If you do not get any indication from God, do not do anything! It is better for us to be killed than for us to kill someone else. If we get killed, God can easily resurrect us. If we murder someone spiritually, we are trapped— not only will we have to apologize to God, but we will have to go and apologize to the other person as well.

brokenness is the key

The process of bringing the soul under the governance of the spirit is called brokenness. This breaking from within is accomplished by the work of the cross. For nineteen years, I did things my way. God, however, had a different plan for my life and worked to break my strength. God does not come to give us strength; He comes to break it and lead our souls into weakness. Jesus said, "So the last will be first, and the first last. For many are called, but few chosen" (Matthew 20:16). When our souls have been wrestled to the floor, our spirits can step up and be seen. God wants to break our power and deliver us into a place where our weakness is welcomed.

In brokenness, what commonly occurs first is dependence on the nature of God. Our relationships become one of worship, thanksgiving and acceptance of His right to rule.

Second, our hearts change toward others (see Figure 3), and our attitudes and approaches to people begin to be adjusted. We start learning to love other people. Typically, this is very difficult and takes quite an internal battle. Unless our attitudes toward ourselves are radically changed (this is normally the last area to be adjusted), then our love is often conditional and

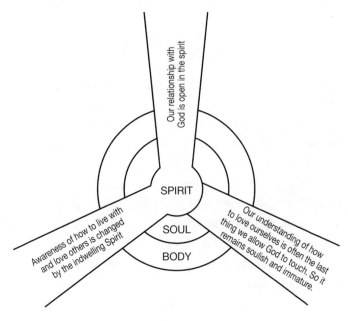

Figure 3

based on another's performance. Also, where there is no self-love, our love for others is limited.

Three times in his epistles, Paul prayed and asked God to remove a "thorn" in his flesh. He had at least three sessions of begging God to take it away from him. He needed these three sessions, because he refused to hear God saying no the first two times. God wanted Paul to understand that His strength is made perfect in His servant's weakness. Finally, Paul understood the lesson:

> And lest I should be exalted above measure by the abundance of the revelations, a thorn in the flesh was given to me, a messenger of Satan to buffet me, lest I be exalted above measure. Concerning this thing I pleaded with the Lord three times that it might depart from me. And He said to me, "My grace is sufficient for you, for My strength is made perfect in weakness." Therefore most gladly I will rather boast in my infirmities, that the power of Christ may rest upon me. Therefore I take pleasure in infirmities, in reproaches, in needs, in persecutions, in distresses, for Christ's sake. For when I am weak, then I am strong.
>
> 2 Corinthians 12:7–10

When we learn to enjoy our weakness, an expectancy that God is going to work on our behalf is birthed. Usually the first thing God seeks to break in the lives of Christians is our attitudes toward other people. The Holy Spirit rushes in, and we start thinking about other people. He touches our souls and begins to change our hearts, and we discover how to love others truly. A soul touched by God loves Him and is drawn to Him in relationship. That shift prompts the same soul to love others.

> "The guidance of the Spirit is generally by gentle suggestions or drawings, and not in violent pushes; and it requires great childlikeness of heart to be faithful to it. The secret of being made willing lies in a definite giving up of our will. As soon as we put our will on to God's side, He immediately takes possession of it and begins to work in us to will and to do of His good pleasure."
> —Hannah Whitall Smith

It is possible to be touched by God but not changed—Samson and Solomon are two examples of this point. Samson's life was anointed by God, but his lifestyle was just one indiscretion after another. God raised him up to be a champion of the nation, to deliver Israel from her enemies. Instead, Samson wound up as a laughingstock—a bald, blind and bound prisoner of the very people he was called to defeat.

Samson's only recourse was to pull down an entire building, killing himself and as many enemies as he could. Was this God's plan for Samson? I doubt it. I think God had a grander purpose for his life, but Samson's soulishness led him into disaster.

Solomon had a tremendous relationship with God. "Ask me for anything you want, and I'll give it to you," God said to him in a dream. Solomon asked for wisdom, and the Lord gave him that and everything else he could ever have dreamed of. Solomon fulfilled his father's dream and built a temple for God. Can you imagine what it must have been like on the day the temple was dedicated? The presence of God was so thick that it must have been impossible to stand. A nation did some carpet time!

With all of this communication with God, how could Solomon have ended up so bitter, so distracted by his lust? He was a king who started radiantly but finished in darkness. He was touched, but not changed, by God because he refused to allow his soul's power to be broken.

A soul in charge of its own spirituality often becomes religious and Pharisaical. It creates hundreds of rules for people, all meant to keep everything under control. The soul will manipulate everything it can to keep its reign intact. It uses people but does not release them. A soulish relationship is conditional, based on appearances and what a person can deliver.

Brokenness occurs gradually. We wish we could get it all done in a single weekend, moving from soulishness to spirit-led life in three easy steps. But it does not work that way—it is a process. We have to learn powerlessness in order to receive power. We have to learn weakness and helplessness in order to gain authority.

> "We have to learn powerlessness in order to receive power. We have to learn weakness and helplessness in order to gain authority."

When God breaks us, He breaks us wide open. In that shattered mirror, we see who we are supposed to be. The soul, which has been hiding that true life from us, is broken and out of the way. At that moment, there is a lightening of the spirit that happens—for the first time, we see who God has called us to be. It is an incredible moment that makes all the pain, rejection, humiliation and betrayal we have faced worthwhile.

When Joseph's brothers sold the young dreamer into slavery, he had a choice—he could live in a twisted and hateful way, or he could choose to be healed of that rejection. He chose to let his spirit guide his life. When his brothers, years later, stood before him, desperate and penitent, Joseph absolved them of all responsibility. He said, "But now, do not therefore be grieved or angry with yourselves because you sold me here; for God sent me before you to preserve life" (Genesis 45:5). Joseph's soul was broken before the Lord, and he was able to see what God was telling his spirit.

In Genesis 32 we read that Jacob had to wrestle with an angel to have something broken and come under the rule of God. The angel wrenched his hip out of its socket, leaving Jacob to limp the rest of his life as a physical manifestation of spiritual brokenness.

We must understand that God has to break our capacity for self-rule. The true word of the cross is Jesus' prayer in Gethsemane, "Nevertheless not My will, but Yours, be done" (Luke 22:42). The only form of control acceptable in the Church is self-control. A great church leadership team should bring its parishioners to a place where the parishioners govern their own lives. If we have to be governed by our church leadership, there is something wrong with us. The role of leaders is to serve the purpose of God in the company they are part of and to facilitate people to come into a deeper relationship with God so the people can govern themselves.

"A great church leadership team should bring its parishioners to a place where the parishioners govern their own lives."

Self-governed people who choose to submit their souls to their spirits do not have to talk about commitment. They are doing it, being it, enjoying it. We must open our lives to the spirit, seeing the fruit of the Holy Spirit, and especially self-control, ripen.

What is God breaking? He is breaking our dominating, manipulative self. He is breaking the tendency to use our intelligence to intimidate people. He is breaking the desire to use physical size to domineer. He is breaking this, in all its forms and subtlety. He is breaking the way some people can destroy a room with a look. He is breaking anything not of the spirit.

God is calling us to learn to become humble and submissive to Him. He is calling us, once the soul has been submitted to the spirit, to put it in proper order— will first, which affects our minds and touches our emotions. Soulish people always put their wills last, while spiritual people put their wills first in the order of the soul. Reasserting the will is a vehicle of the spirit. The will enables us to develop our minds into the mind of Christ. Having the mind of Christ is where we constantly give our thinking over to God, instinctively and intuitively thinking of something the same way God thinks of it. We can then see life from God's perspective.

All Christians are children of God, but it is our capacity of suffering that leads us into the path of experiencing His glory through sonship. We are all children, all heirs of God, but if we do not win the battle of spirit over soul, we will never inherit the fullness of God. Like Israel in her first trip around the desert, we will be able to see only glimpses of the Promised Land until we bow our knee to God's authority.

> "Satan trembles when he sees the weakest saint upon his knees."
> —William Cowper

love yourself and others

Brokenness feels very risky to pursue, but it is the only way to a truly blessed life. Until our true self is released to be loved and accepted, it will protect itself from harm—and the best form of protection is usually to attack someone else. Knock them down a peg to lift yourself up. Most of us have built a defensive perimeter through our life experiences. This is what psychologists call learned behavior. We do not trust other people, which usually translates into a mistrust of God.

Self-acceptance is the key to loving others. It is vital that we have the right opinion of ourselves. To do that, we need to know what God has saved us from and the work He still wants to do in our lives. We must be realistic in our assessments of our lives: *I am where I am in God, and I like being there. I know God has more to change, but by His grace I'm going to make it. I love the fact that I love where I am with God right now. I know what He wants to change next and I am doing my best to cooperate.*

Until "self" is released to be loved and accepted, it will protect itself from harm. The true self, wrapped up in the spirit and living in the love and pleasure of God,

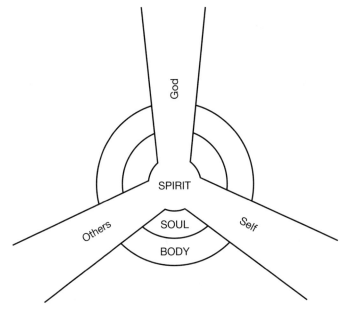

Figure 4

is completely unafraid of being hurt. "There is no fear in love; but perfect love casts out fear, because fear involves torment. But he who fears has not been made perfect in love. We love Him because He first loved us" (1 John 4:18–19). Figure 4 illustrates this aspect of brokenness.

Most of the teaching on love in the Church centers on loving God or other people. Very little of it talks about loving ourselves. We have been taught how to subjugate ourselves, but not how to love ourselves without being selfish. Loving ourselves out of our souls is selfish; loving ourselves because of what God has done in our spirits is beautiful. Most Christians have never learned that distinction.

If the Spirit of Christ does not rule over our souls, we will always require reassurance about our relationships with God. *I don't know if God loves me,* we will moan. *I think He's angry with me. He's fed up with me. I've messed up so many times—I'll never be anything for Him.*

We must hear God when He tells us that He likes us. As we mature in Him, we will hear that more and more, in different ways. "I like you," He says. "I love you 100 percent." Whenever we respond to His touch and change our ways to be more like His, He'll like us again—it never wavers. He has plans to change us, but He is happy with where we are.

In relationships with others, human nature is to

withhold part of ourselves. We are naturally wary, willing to wait and see how the other person responds to our tiniest of gestures. We give ourselves partially. Church leaders, meanwhile, preach endlessly about commitment and loyalty—there is a disconnection between the two groups. When people are not taught how to love themselves, they cannot experience the freedom that stability brings.

In my church in Southampton, England, the role of our leadership team is to help every one of our people to become the fullest expression of Christ that they can become. We want to set people free to be who they are in God, to serve Him as fully as they want to. I do not expect, as a leader, to be in control of that process—I expect to be a facilitator.

People have so many reasons for not letting God be God in their lives. Their excuses for soulish behavior never cease: "I've been burned before," some people say. "Once bitten, twice shy." That kind of thought actually shuts out the one Person who can heal you—God.

God wants to come in and touch our true selves, removing all barriers and shame. He wants to flow through us, intentionally doing us good. He will overwhelm every hurdle we put up to protect ourselves from people and situations. Through His love for us, He will heal our

> "I sometimes have a bright dream of reunion engulfing us unawares, like a great wave from behind our backs— perhaps at the very moment when our official representatives are still pronouncing it impossible. Discussions usually separate us; actions sometimes unite us."
> —C. S. Lewis

fear of being wounded by others. When our spirits rule our souls, our attitude toward others shifts. "I know I can give you something," becomes our motto. We begin to love everybody, even blessing our own enemies, as Jesus preached: "But I say to you, love your enemies, bless those who curse you, do good to those who hate you, and pray for those who spitefully use you and persecute you, that you may be sons of your Father in heaven" (Matthew 5:44–45).

grace and mercy

A spiritual Christian passes the kindness and mercy of God to others. There is more kindness of God over our lives than we'll ever be able to use. Even if we are wildly extravagant, there's more kindness available. We are swimming in His love for us! God overwhelms His children with His grace. With this kindness available, we are able to forget past issues. There is no condemnation in Christ, only a Friend who is there to help us process things and move on. God wants to love the true you and see it emerge. He speaks to the treasure in us.

His grace and mercy woo our hearts. God gave us the fruit of the Spirit so we can have the fun of being like Him. Love, joy, peace, longsuffering, kindness, goodness, faithfulness, gentleness, self-control—this is how He lives His life and how He wants us to live ours.

All these gifts emerge from the inner person to be spread through the soul toward as many people as possible.

The only cure for a closed heart is a revelation of the real love of God. Nothing but His unconditional love can reach anyone. We always know where we stand with God because He never changes. His feelings for us never waver. We always have a place in His affections; we are always welcome in His home. The confidence that comes with His love is part of our inheritance—we must accept it. God does not speak to our flesh, because He killed that at Calvary. He speaks to the Jesus in us because that is the value Jesus gives us before the Father. His sacrifice has made a way for us to come into God's presence at any time. He has all the power in the world, and He loves us—this should make anyone confident.

> "The only cure for a closed heart is a revelation of the real love of God."

soul power and soulish nature

The soul touched by God loves Him! It is drawn to Him but wants the relationship on its own terms—the soul wants to be in charge. This has to be broken through a process of submission and surrender, the work of the cross.

There is a form of surrender that is soulish, not spiritual. We become religious when we manage our spirituality. With religiosity comes control, and with control comes the desire to dominate. This leads to others being condemned and judged if they do not see things our way.

How much of our "spirituality" is threatened by opposition? Do we feel the urge to control or dominate in human confrontations? How much of our peace is destroyed by conflict? How easily upset are we? How long does it take us to regain normal, good humor? How vulnerable are we to anger, resentment and bitterness? How long do we hold a grudge? How quick are we to forgive? How willing are we to be restored?

If the answer to any of those questions is, in any way, negative, we are more likely living in our souls than in our spirits.

God is breaking our controlling selves by enabling us to submit to the spiritual fruit of self-control. Our dominating, manipulative selves must become humble and submissive to Christ. We must learn to reassert our wills as the vehicle of the spirit over our emotions and thought lives.

We are learning to renew our minds in the spirit so that we might think as God thinks about people and situations. The soul is governed by the mind of Christ. We learn to develop faith to rule our feelings so that we are not always fluctuating between doubt and trust. We learn to kill our Pharisaical religiosity through the joyful imposition of unconditional love.

converted person

Earlier, we looked at what an unregenerate person looks like; now, I would like to give a picture of the converted person. Conversion brings us into the presence of God; the whole point of church is to maintain that presence and teach people how to abide in it. Jesus said, "If you abide in Me, and My words abide in you, you will ask what you desire, and it shall be done for you" (John 15:7). Whatever we want, He will do, if we are abiding in Him—that is power!

Jesus, according to 1 Corinthians 15, is a life-giving Spirit sent to regenerate our spiritual beings. The new birth He told Nicodemus about (see John 3) means that the human spirit can be recreated and restored to a living relationship with God. When that salvation occurs, the spirit must be restored to its place of primacy over the soul. When the soul gives up its power to rule and the human spirit is filled with the Holy Spirit, the power of God is released to sanctify and bring harmony to all of the faculties of the soul.

This harmony can be called "wholeness." Scripture speaks of wholeness in several places. When we read that a person was made whole, we interpret that to mean a physical healing. But God is more concerned with wholeness than with healing. Healing is just a part of being made whole. When Jesus prayed for people and they were made whole, they didn't just get healed of their ailments—their entire being was made whole.

To be saved, the soul must come to the cross, not to be destroyed but to give up its right to rule. Only then can it be liberated. Salvation, then, is a process—we have been saved; we are being saved; we will be saved. We need to examine our lives constantly and see what parts of them need to go before the cross, be saved and be brought under the rule of God. It is one thing to make Jesus our Savior but a completely different thing to make Him our Lord.

> "I think it must hurt the tender love of our Father when we press for reasons for his dealings with us, as though he were not Love, as though not he but another chose our inheritance for us, and as though what he chose to allow could be less than the very best and dearest that Love Eternal had to give."
> —Amy Carmichael

The soul does not fully comprehend the ways of God. It has no wisdom; only knowledge. That knowledge is forged by previous experience and can plateau at a certain level and remain there for years. The spirit, however, can interact with God's wisdom through revelation. Revelation unfolds the mysteries of God as we progress in our spiritual journeys. The soul is subject to that revelation and mystery but cannot perceive either; only the spirit can. Submission increases our vision and capacity to see in the realm of the spirit.

Our spirits are intended to give us access to divine

wisdom, which allows us to direct our lives according to the will of God. Humanity was never intended to have independent resources of wisdom through which to operate our own lives. We are very clever, but a lot of that cleverness leads to destruction. We need God's wisdom to keep that cleverness from being dangerous. Our brilliance has led us, for example, to rape the planet, using up its resources and polluting it at an astonishing and sickening rate. Humanity is highly intelligent, but without the wisdom of God, we act insanely.

Wisdom is the ability to choose right goals and achieve them through godly means. God gives us that wisdom, and it can be found in our spirits. Knowledge lives in our heads, but the wisdom of God flows from our spirits. Our level of wisdom, therefore, is not dependent on intelligence, education, common sense, experience, culture or age. These are all valid forms of knowledge, but they are not the wisdom that comes from God.

> "What is 'spirit'? Spirit is: to live as though dead [dead to the world]."
> —Søren Kierkegaard

Because of this access to divine wisdom, God ordained the human spirit to be the part of our beings that directs us. God's order is clear—the Holy Spirit rules our spirits, our spirits rule our minds and our minds rule our bodies. Adam was given dominion over all creation, based on this divine order. In the Garden of

Eden, he and Eve were perfectly whole with no opening for sin or sickness to creep in. The enemy in his deviousness, however, subverted Adam's and Eve's spirits to come under soulish desires and wrecked God's perfect order.

Spiritual people use their souls as vehicles for their spirits. They take what is happening internally, what God is revealing to them, and use the soul to reveal it outwardly. The soul was meant as a link between body and spirit. It is designed to fulfill our destinies of introducing the wisdom and values of the spiritual realm to the natural world.

Spirit life knows where the source of wholeness lies— God. When we live in our souls, we are always sitting around, waiting for something to happen. We are like the man who lay by the pool of Bethesda and waited 38 years to be healed. Jesus arrived on the scene and asked him if he wanted to get well. Sometimes, we do not want to be healed—we'd rather wear our pain like a cloak.

"Not only do we not know God except through Jesus Christ; we do not even know ourselves except through Jesus Christ."
—Blaise Pascal

A soulish man sits and waits for something to happen, but a spiritual man knows that God is always working. "No need to wait," a spirit-led Christian says. "I just need to find out what God wants to do today and get in on it." We are our own revival when we live the way God wants us to live.

adopted by God

As the Holy Spirit intermingles with our spirits, a quickening takes place. At that moment, a divine acceleration can occur. As the soul dies to itself, the spirit's life flourishes. People who are led by the Spirit are true representatives of God. They are the very sons and daughters of God.

God wants to put us into a place of sonship, a deep relationship with Him where power and authority can flow. He longs to "adopt" us, but not in the way we use the word in the modern, Western world. It is not about taking someone who is not your child and bringing them into your family; we are all born again of the Spirit and are already children of the Father. God does not want legally bought children—He wants love-bought children. Adoption, in ancient Hebrew times, was a ceremony that marked a rite of passage for a son, where his male parent went from being "Daddy" to a more mature "Father." Adoption is about moving from childlike immaturity to a more compelling, fuller relationship with God as the Lord of our lives.

The adoption ceremony always involved the community. A son would grow up in his daddy's house, taking on more responsibility as he got older, learning to be trustworthy and faithful. Daddy would correct him here and there, and eventually the child would come to the place where he could be trusted. At that moment, the father would call for a ceremony of adoption in the village square and put on a big feast. In the midst of the party, Daddy would stand up and call his son forward. In front of the whole community, he would say, "This is my son, in whom I am well pleased." At that moment, the son became like the father. If he wrote a check, the dad would honor it. If the boy gave his word, it was as if the father himself had spoken. A son's promise committed the father. The boy could act and speak for the father. He was the father's fully mature son. The community's demeanor toward the child shifted after the feast. From that moment on they would treat the son the same way they treated the father.

> "This is my son, in whom I am well pleased."

I would love to see this ceremony of adoption come back into the Church as a rite of passage. Imagine a generation of men and women being mentored and then released at the same level as their mentors. What do we have now in the Church? Membership. People's names are put on a roll, and they are given a tithe number. It is heartbreaking.

An adoption ceremony would be so much fuller. Bringing an equipped, loved and proven person forward and releasing that person in front of the entire Church community is so much richer than a membership card.

We should be releasing our sons, laying hands on them and recognizing their ministries. Adoption was a communal recognition of a relational truth. This is what should happen when we set out elders or deacons. The person should be recognized, respected and released to lead.

> "The Son of God is the teacher of men, giving to them of His Spirit—that Spirit which manifests the deep things of God, being to a man the mind of Christ."
> —George Macdonald

The spirit of adoption enables our relationship with God to change from *abba* (Aramaic, with the connotation "daddy") to *pater* (Greek for "father"). We move from immaturity to maturity, as God leads us through the process. We move away from being children toward being His sons. To do this takes the breaking of our soulish natures. We must live our lives in the spirit, proving ourselves to the Father.

When we commission people for ministry, we are doing the same thing—recognizing their gifts, growth, maturity and integrity. The real anointing of God is only bestowed in sonship because it is a relational thing. In Southampton, we wouldn't dream of releasing someone into ministry unless we had a relational connection with him or her, because we do not want to see people as functions. We want to know them, to see them grow, to see them mature into their fullest expression of God. Then we can release them before the whole church, and their anointing will be recognized by our community.

conclusion

To live in the glory of God, we must walk the pathway of submitting our souls to our spirits. We must take our thoughts captive and control our emotions. Our wills must move to center stage, deciding to submit to the power of our spirits. If our emotions are dominant, we won't feel like doing this. If our intellects control us, we'll think up a way to get out of it. The will must take command of the soul. Paul wrote, "Work out your own salvation with fear and trembling, for it is God who works in you both to will and to do for His good pleasure" (Philippians 2:12–13).

God wants to activate our wills so they can dominate our thinking and our feeling. Our wills push the soul under the spirit, allowing God to shine through and do what He wants to do. Exercising the will is a cold-blooded act: *I will do this thing. No matter what I feel, I'll do it.*

As we use our wills to force our souls to submit, it becomes easier and easier to do. Our faith in God grows as we see what He is doing around us. As David sings:

> I would have lost heart, unless I had believed
> That I would see the goodness of the LORD
> In the land of the living.
>
> Psalm 27:13

Our wills allow us to see how big God can be and help us to trust that the Holy Spirit will make us more like Jesus.

When the soul comes under the rule of the spirit, life and peace are the result. Suddenly, we do not have to know everything—we just become wise about where to stand at any given moment. We do not know how everything will pan out, but we learn to be happy with the process of getting there. We become fixated on holding God's hand and do not worry about the trouble around us.

God does, at times, lift our eyes up to the horizon and reveal where we are going. But when He does not, a spiritual man or woman should still be content, happy to walk out His journey step by step. This walk of faith is wonderful. Sometimes, God keeps us from seeing what is down the road because He is jealous for our love. He wants us to be fully preoccupied with Him. Other times, He opens the windows and we can see into the future. God will always give us the right amount of light, whether it be for the next step of our journey or for the next hundred miles.

God has so much more for us than the soulish lives we have lived. His Spirit longs to mingle with our own, giving us the wisdom, revelation, assurance and love that will develop us into amazing spiritual beings. The first step is to use our wills to choose to come under our spirits' rule. This is the beginning of His dream for us.

Jesus is Lord

Beloved. You resist the enemy not by fighting his mind forays but by submitting to the mind of Christ within. Learn to turn and yield your thoughts to Mine. Practice will enable you to take thoughts captive.

The place of deliverance is within you. It is the safe and holy place of the inner man of your spirit, where My life rules and reigns supreme. In this delightful discipline, I will create a fortress in your mind as you cooperate with Me.

There is an equalizing pressure within that not only disregards enemy attacks on the mind but also delivers a positive truth and perspective to counter enemy assaults on your life and others around you.

In this next season, the battle for your mind and thought life will intensify because this is the time of your appointed breakthrough.

I am going to enable you to enjoy peace of mind. As you give away your worries, anxieties and fears, you will experience an eternal victory that is being shaped and influenced by holy thinking.

chart 1

What is the soul?	What is the spirit?
Mind	Shares the mind of Christ
Will	Surrenders to the cross
Emotions	Comes under trust and faith
The outer man	The inner man
The outer being	The inner being
A vehicle for the spirit	A vehicle for the Holy Spirit
Fruit from the Tree of the Knowledge of Good and Evil	Fruit from the Tree of Life
Controls the body	Controls the soul
Wants self-gratification	Subject to God
Martha (Luke 10:38-42)	Mary (Luke 10:38-42)
Cain (Genesis 4)	Abel (Genesis 4)
Carnal	Spiritual
Can live in religiosity	Can only live by the Holy Spirit
Preoccupied with the first heaven	Preoccupied with the third heaven
Always seeking reassurance	Knows its home in the love of God
Performance Christianity	Passionate Christianity
Wants status, position, fame	Seeks humility, rest, obscurity

chart 2

What is the first heaven?	The earth, the physical realm where our souls and bodies operate
What is the second heaven?	Where Satan and his demonic forces operate, the kingdom of evil and darkness
What is the third heaven?	Where God's throne room resides, accessible by our spirits intermingling with the Holy Spirit, the Kingdom of God and light

A Meeting: In the Secret Place

Come and join me
I'm drawing you into a quiet place
Of introspection
Come away from the noise
Into the place of stillness.

No, beloved, I'm not talking of externals
I'm not speaking of a physical place that you need to reach.

There is a safe place within you,
A quiet place. Where stillness reigns.
I'm asking you to retreat from the soul
Your Martha of many distractions
Legitimate, powerful, necessary, but ultimately unhelpful
… compared to what I want to give you.

Step back into your spirit
Through the inner fortress of your heart
Away from the world and the busyness of your soul.

Meet the Mary that is your spirit person
And come to sit at My feet.

I'm here, in the secret place of your spirit,
Waiting.
All you need is here by Me.

Provision, peace and a rest for your soul
Come and sit quietly by Me.

I am the pool of water by your feet
I am the manna falling
I am the raven feeding you
The tree of life that gives you shade
I am the gentle breeze that kisses your brow
I am the eagle's cry, watching over you from above

I am the velvet paws of the lion padding protectively around your camp.

Step back, far back into your spirit
Practice being still, learn the way of peace.

I will deal with the issues
Remove the spots and blemishes
Refine your heart.

I will empty you of all that you don't need and never wanted
I will purge and purify your heart.

I will imprison Eros and release Agape within you.
All self-obsession, ambition, preservation
Will die in you
I will empty you of all that grieves Me and frustrates you
And fill the vacuum with worship.

Out of that place of internal rest
Will come a new creation
Soft, pliable
Owning nothing yet possessing all things.

A servant will merge with the son,
A warrior will grow out of the child,
Action will flow out of rest
In the secret place of your spirit.

The enemy cannot find you,
The vagaries of life, leave you untouched,
Impurities will be drawn away from your heart
In the quiet strength of My presence.

The aching, the longing in your heart
Will be overshadowed by all My desire for you.
You shall be fully known
And you will know.

appendix 1

Resting in God

What you have to focus on now is the incomparable love of God for you. Right now, where you are, He adores you. He couldn't love you any more than He loves you at this very moment. This is the thing He wants to plant in your heart: "I love you, I've always loved you and I always will love you. I love you 100 percent, right now. Be at peace."

There is no good time to learn about resting, for something will always try to prevent you from resting. Psalm 46 opens with an earthquake and ends with "Be still, and know that I am God." Mark 4 has a storm threatening the safety and security of the disciples. The antidote is to speak peace, as Jesus does. But if you can rest now, you can rest at any other time. God has given you permission to rest when you are in turmoil about yourself. What are you resting in? You are resting in the fact that God adores you, right now. You are resting in His ability to change you all the time. And you are resting in the fact that you are totally acceptable to Him. It does not matter what is occurring around or within you—you are acceptable in Christ. So rest.

Study Jesus' words: "Come to Me, all you who labor and are heavy laden, and I will give you rest. Take My yoke upon you and learn from Me, for I am gentle and lowly in heart, and you will find rest for your souls. For My yoke is easy and My burden is light" (Matthew 11:28–30). A yoke is a harness that fits over the shoulders. It connects us to the one walking alongside and enables us to move in unison. Jesus has promised us that if we walk with Him, we can bear our burdens in a completely different manner. What would the freedom to rest really bring us in our busy lives?

Let the Father's peace fall in your life, a peace that transcends all understanding. Ask the Lord to come and wash your mind in His peace. Let it fall on you. Pray that the Prince of Peace would come to you. Ask Him to take away worry, fear, doubt, self-loathing, self-hatred, your masks and your pretenses, leaving only peace in their place. He first loved us, and with Him we will win this battle of spirit over soul. It is going to be a good fight, but our spirits are going to win.

Identify your current unrest or lack of peace. What are you not seeing about God's power or faithfulness? Does your lack of peace arise out of a wrong perception? What needs to change so that peace may remain? Sometimes peace is restored by the simple act of pushing away worry, fear, anxiety, panic and unbelief. Try it. Get tough on the causes of unrest within yourself. The writer of Hebrews calls it laboring to enter that rest (see Hebrews 4:8–11). We have to work at being at peace!

appendix 2

dealing with disillusionment

It is impossible for God to become disillusioned with us—He never had any illusions about us in the first place. The Lord knows exactly who each of us is. On the day we came to Him, we couldn't have been in a worse state. He saw us at rock bottom. And still He pursued, found and kissed us. He loved us 100 percent then and still does now. We have no reason to hide from His love.

When we live in our souls, we always look for reassurance. Our grip on our relationship with God is always shaky; we feel like we need constant ministry to hold on to it. We feel like we do not really belong to Him. But the problem is not that God has illusions about us—it is that we have illusions about Him!

We often ascribe human qualities to God, rather than divine ones. *God must be really annoyed with me,* we think. *How could He ever forgive me?*

Years ago, I came to the Lord and said, *I'm sorry. I keep coming back to You with the same issue.*

What issue? He replied. *This is the first time you've come to Me with this.*

No, I did it yesterday, Lord.

Oh, I forgot all about that, He said. *That was yesterday, and it's under the blood of Christ—it no longer speaks of failure.*

My daughter, Sophie, says God has a memory like a thousand elephants, except when it comes to sin. If we have repented, our sin is under the blood, and He has forgotten all about it. Our souls cannot accept that sometimes, because we are subject to doubt, fear, insecurity and unbelief. We also become disillusioned with one another.

I once had a man come to me and tell me he was disillusioned with me. "Thank God for that!" I said. "Disillusionment is the breaking of our illusions. You had illusions about me, and now they're broken. That means we can have a real relationship based on truth, not illusion. We can enter into reality together."

I have friends who know what I am like on a good day and know what I am like on a bad day. They know the areas where I am tempted to sin. They know it all because they ask me very awkward questions. But we have given each other that right. My life is incredibly safe because of the fact that I have people who love me whether I am doing well or badly. This is real friendship.

Disillusionment is a stage we go through in order to get real. It brings us to deeper communion and friendship. It rips away our veneers of respectability. We all wear masks and hide behind an image of ourselves. Real friendship gets behind that mask. We must get disillusioned with one another and move on into reality. Kleenex relationships, where we use one another and then throw one another away, are ruining the Church.

When we meet men and women ruled by the spirit, there is a humility that reaches out and touches us. Their brokenness moves us. Their gentleness, meekness, peace touch us powerfully. We feel at ease with such people and are able to share ourselves—the masks slip away.

With soulish people, the mask stays firmly in place. Instinctively, we know that if they see behind our masks, they will kill us spiritually. But as long as we remain soulish, we remain in bondage. Our belief systems cannot be truly changed as long as we persist in soulish behavior. We will live in the illusions we have about ourselves and others.

Questions for Meditation

1. Regarding past relationships that did not work out: Have you ever experienced disillusionment over someone?
   a. What illusions did you have that were broken?
   b. Did you let go of the relationship because of this?

   c. In what way could you have seen him or her and the situation differently?

   d. What would need to change in you in order for you to see him or her as God does?

   e. If disillusionment is a doorway into a deeper reality, what fruit(s) of the Spirit must be established in you so that your enhanced vision can create a deeper place of understanding/empathy to improve your relationships?

   f. How will you enable this to happen through your cooperation with the Holy Spirit?

2. Are you disillusioned with God?

   a. What is it about your perception of God that is not working for you?

   b. What is the place within that the Holy Spirit is seeking to build so that a greater sense of His presence can be found?

   c. What is the conflict within you that requires a deeper peace and a greater revelation of truth?

   d. What is the Father's vision of you that forms part of the "truth that sets you free"?

   e. If repentance is about changing your mind-set, what *old* thinking must you delete from your mind and what *new* thoughts must be established through everyday experience?

   f. If revelation is a springboard to experience, what new expectations of God is the Holy Spirit developing in your life?

g. How will this new experience/expectation affect your lifestyle of faith and your thinking about the future?

3. Regarding hard relationships: Explain how you will look at current friendships and the possibility of new relationships from a more spiritual perspective.

   a. Who can you be "real" with? Name people.

   b. How can you demonstrate to these people that you want to see them differently?

   c. Can you see beyond the masks they wear? How can you appreciate and value them as people struggling to conform to Jesus?

   d. How can you let your own mask drop and how can you develop more trusting relationships with your friends?

4. What is unconditional, non-negotiable love like, in your view?

   a. How can you experience it in Christ?

   b. How can you minister it to others?

   c. What is your own internal place of safety in Christ (your refuge/high tower) from which you can experience and be changed by such love?

   d. How do you plan to locate and use such love on behalf of other people?

appendix 3

Where there is no self-love, our love for others is limited and often conditional. This is the heart of what I call "performance Christianity." Many Christians live with a sense of unworthiness. Our true selves are still imprisoned, slaves to do things that will win us acceptance or approval. We have not let ourselves out of the jail Jesus came to free us from.

When Jesus came out of the wilderness after forty days, He immediately began to speak about His ministry. Before that test, He had been with the people, sharing about God. After the test, He went to the Church of the day to announce His ministry. He went immediately to a company of people who thought they belonged to God. When He got there, He read Isaiah 61:1:

> The Spirit of the LORD GOD is upon Me,
> Because the LORD has anointed Me
> To preach good tidings to the poor;

> He has sent Me to heal the brokenhearted,
> To proclaim liberty to the captives,
> And the opening of the prison to those who are bound.

The prisoner He came to free was the Church of His day.

Sometimes I think there are more people bound inside the Church than there are outside it. Bound by Pharisaical behavior, by religiosity, by a system that does not set them free to be who they are in God. We have become conformed not to God but to the religious system of our day. We find lots of teachers telling us what to do, but very few fathers releasing us to learn how to become sons. And we wonder why people leave the Church in droves!

I love the Church, with all of her flaws, idiosyncrasies and weirdness. There is no plan B for God—the Church is all we have. We have to find a way to become a company of people who gladden the heart of God together and are intensely supernatural in the earth.

"The opening of the prison to those who are bound." Jesus spoke those words to the Church of His day, and He speaks them to us again. To win this battle against performance Christianity, we must learn to love ourselves and to love God and our neighbors as fully as that. The problem is that we already love our neighbors as we love ourselves—we do not like ourselves, and we have little patience for other people.

Performance Christians pray and give to be seen.

Everything is about appearance and being noticed. The soul is not broken in these people. While the soul wants recognition in the form of status, position, titles and fame, the spirit is content just to live in the presence of God. We must get into our spirit.

Paul wrote, "For those who live according to the flesh set their minds on the things of the flesh, but those who live according to the Spirit, the things of the Spirit. For to be carnally minded is death, but to be spiritually minded is life and peace" (Romans 8:5–6). Those who live in their soul can please God periodically, but not continually. The spirit man, however, can dwell in Him, and He in the spirit man. We must have that Spirit of Christ.

People who live in the soul seldom have clear victories—there is always something left undone and no real ground is taken. They battle over the same issue again and again. Performance Christians have no progression in their lives—they are up and down over everything.

A performance mentality seeks to earn a relationship with God through activity. Scripture talks about faith and works (in that order). Our faith is justified when we act on what we believe about God and ourselves. God's love enables. God's power releases. His life within develops our lifestyles without. He is the Creator, the Architect, the Builder. All flows from Him. His life moves from the inside to the outside of our lives.

Our relationship *with* God is the motivating factor. We love others in the way that we are loved by the Lord. We serve the Lord out of gratitude for all He is and all He has done in our lives. We are not trying to get anywhere with God—we recognize that in Christ we are already there, *and* in our experience of grace we are also becoming more of who we really are in Christ. It is a wonderful paradox that sets us free to be and to become.

Performance Christians live in the opposite manner, doing everything to feel accepted and acceptable to God. They think that attending meetings, praying more, witnessing, serving and reading the Bible more will bring them closer to God. No, our relationship with the Father is based on what Christ has already accomplished on the cross. We are already accepted in the beloved (see Ephesians 1). There is nothing we can do to earn God's love. Grace and mercy are poured out upon us constantly as part of our salvation gift.

We have more grace and mercy than we can conceivably use for ourselves, so we can allow it to be poured through us to others. In this way, we are true representatives of the Father's heart to all people.

Performance-oriented people have little patience or love for others. They see faults rather than potential. They condemn sin rather than release mercy. They speak truth without grace. They rely on self-effort rather than acceptance in Christ as the foundation for their experience. However, they rightly express that "Faith without works is dead." But they do not understand that works alone will never bring about all that God seeks to do in us or release through us.

The fact is that we pray, witness, serve, read Scripture and attend meetings not to reach out to God but to express our sheer enjoyment that He is reaching out to us. It is how we celebrate His love. He is with us, He is for us and we wriggle with the pleasure of His joy in us. He sings over us. He laughs at our enemies. He forgives so readily. He understands us completely.

In the spirit, we learn to live every day under His smile. Our soul strives for the acceptance our spirit so readily receives.

Questions for Meditation

1. Do you struggle with accepting who you are in Christ?
   a. How easy do you find it to trust in all the Father has provided for you in Jesus?
   b. What are your major barriers to self-acceptance?
   c. Do your emotions run the show in terms of your spirituality? For example, if your emotions were running counter to what you should believe, which would dominate?

d. What is the effect of your non-acceptance in Christ on your other relationships?

e. Do you feel you need to do anything to earn God's love or approval?

f. What is preventing you from living as a much-loved child before the Father?

appendix 4

lectio divina

Lectio Divina (Latin for "Divine Reading") is an ancient way of reading the Bible—allowing a quiet and contemplative way of coming to God's Word. Lectio Divina opens the pulse of the Scripture, helping readers dig far deeper into the Word than normally happens in a quick glance-over.

In this exercise, we will look at a portion of Scripture and use a modified Lectio Divina technique to engage it. This technique can be used on any piece of Scripture; I highly recommend using it for key Bible passages the Lord has highlighted for you and for anything you think might be an inheritance word for your life (see my book *Crafted Prayer* for more on inheritance words).

There is therefore now no condemnation to those who are in Christ Jesus, who do not walk according to the flesh, but according to the Spirit. For the law of the Spirit of life in Christ Jesus has made me free from the law of sin and death. For what the law could not do in that it was weak through the flesh, God did by sending His own Son in the likeness of sinful flesh, on account of sin: He condemned sin in the flesh, that the righteous requirement of the law might be fulfilled in us who do not walk according to the flesh but according to the Spirit. For those who live according to the flesh set their minds on the things of the flesh, but those who live according to the Spirit, the things of the Spirit. For to be carnally minded is death, but to be spiritually minded is life and peace. Because the carnal mind is enmity against God; for it is not subject to the law of God, nor indeed can be. So then, those who are in the flesh cannot please God. But you are not in the flesh but in the Spirit, if indeed the Spirit of God dwells in you. Now if anyone does not have the Spirit of Christ, he is not His. And if Christ is in you, the body is dead because of sin, but the Spirit is life because of righteousness. But if the Spirit of Him who raised Jesus from the dead dwells in you, He who raised Christ from the dead will also give life to your mortal bodies through His Spirit who dwells in you.

Therefore, brethren, we are debtors—not to the flesh, to live according to the flesh. For if you live according to the flesh you will die; but if by the Spirit you put to death the deeds of the body, you will live. For as many as are led by the Spirit of God, these are sons of God. For you did not receive the spirit of bondage again to fear, but you received the Spirit of adoption by whom we cry out, "Abba, Father." The Spirit Himself bears witness with our spirit that we are children of God, and if children, then heirs—heirs of God and joint heirs with Christ, if indeed we suffer with Him, that we may also be glorified together.

For I consider that the sufferings of this present time are not worthy to be compared with the glory which shall be revealed in us. For the earnest expectation of the creation eagerly waits for the revealing of the sons of God. For the creation was subjected to futility, not willingly, but because of Him who subjected it in hope; because the creation itself also will be delivered from the bondage of corruption into the glorious liberty of the children of God. For we know that the whole creation groans and labors with birth pangs together until now. Not only that, but we also who have the firstfruits of the Spirit, even we ourselves groan within ourselves, eagerly waiting for the adoption, the redemption of our body. For we were saved in this hope, but hope that is seen is not hope; for why does one still hope for what he sees? But if we hope for what we do not see, we eagerly wait for it with perseverance.

Likewise the Spirit also helps in our weaknesses. For we do not know what we should pray for as we ought, but the Spirit Himself makes intercession for us with groanings which cannot be uttered. Now He who searches the hearts knows what the mind of the Spirit is, because He makes intercession for the saints according to the will of God.

And we know that all things work together for good to those who love God, to those who are the called according to His purpose. For whom He foreknew, He also predestined to be conformed to the image of His Son, that He might be the firstborn among many brethren. Moreover whom He predestined, these He also called; whom He called, these He also justified; and whom He justified, these He also glorified.

What then shall we say to these things? If God is for us, who can be against us? He who did not spare His own Son, but delivered Him up for us all, how shall He not with Him also freely give us all things? Who shall bring a charge against God's elect? It is God who justifies. Who is he who condemns? It is Christ who died, and furthermore is also risen, who is even at the right hand of God, who also makes intercession for us. Who shall separate us from the love of Christ? Shall tribulation, or distress, or persecution, or famine, or nakedness, or peril, or sword? As it is written:

> "For Your sake we are killed all day long;
> We are accounted as sheep for the slaughter."

Yet in all these things we are more than conquerors through Him who loved us. For I am persuaded that neither death nor life, nor angels nor principalities nor powers, nor things present nor things to come, nor height nor depth, nor any other created thing, shall be able to separate us from the love of God which is in Christ Jesus our Lord.

Romans 8

1. Find a place of stillness before God. Embrace His peace. Calm your body, breathe slowly—clear your mind of the distractions of life. Ask God to reveal His rest to you. Whisper the word "stillness." This can take some time, but once you are in that place of rest, enjoy it. Worship God out of it.

2. Read the passage twice, slowly.

   a. Allow its words to become familiar to you, to sink into your spirit. Picture Paul's writing this letter—become part of it. Listen for pieces that catch your attention.

   b. Following the reading, meditate upon what you have heard. What stands out? Write it down:

   . . . .

   . . . .

   . . . .

   c. If a word or phrase from the passage seems highlighted to you, write it down:

   . . . .

   . . . .

3. Read the passage twice again.

   a. Like waves crashing onto a shore, let the words of the Scripture crash onto your spirit. What are you discerning? What are you hearing? What are you feeling? Write it down:

   . . . .

   . . . .

   . . . .

b. What is the theme of this passage? Write it down:

. . . .
. . . .
. . . .
. . . .

c. Does this passage rekindle any memories or experiences? Write them down:

. . . .
. . . .
. . . .
. . . .

d. What is the Holy Spirit saying to you? Write it down:

. . . .
. . . .
. . . .
. . . .

4. Read the passage two final times.
   a. Meditate on it.
   b. Is there something God wants you to do with this passage? Is there something He is calling you to? Write it down:

. . . .
. . . .
. . . .
. . . .
. . . .

c. Pray silently. Tell God what this Scripture is leading you to think about. Ask Him for His thoughts. Write down your conversation—as if you and God are sitting in a coffee shop, two old and dear friends, sharing:

. . . .
. . . .
. . . .
. . . .
. . . .

5. Pray and thank God for what He has shared with you. Come back to the passage a few more times over the coming weeks.

about the author

Graham Cooke is married to Heather, and they have three adult children, Ben, Seth and Sophie. Graham and Heather divide their time between Southampton, England, and Vacaville, California.

Graham is a member of the apostolic team of c.net (Cornerstone), a network of ministries and a family of churches spanning 44 nations. He is a member of Community Church in Southampton (UK), responsible for the prophetic and training program, and works with team leader Billy Kennedy. In California, he is part of the pastoral leadership team and works with senior pastor David Crone. He has responsibility for Insight, a training program within the church and for the region.

Graham, a popular conference speaker, is well-known for his training programs on the prophetic, spiritual warfare, intimacy with God, leadership and spirituality. He functions as a consultant within c.net (and beyond), specifically helping churches make the transition from one dimension of calling to a higher level of vision and ministry. He has a passion to build prototype churches that can fully reach our postmodern society.

A strong part of Graham's ministry is in producing finances and resources to help the poor, and he

supports many projects around the world. He also
financially supports and helps to underwrite church
planting, leadership development, evangelism and
health and rescue projects in the developing world. If
you wish to become a financial partner for the sake of
missions, please contact Graham's office, where his
personal assistant, Carole Shiers, will be able to assist
you.

Graham has many prayer partners who play a
significant part in his ministry. For more information,
check his website (below).

Graham has written four other books, *Developing
Your Prophetic Gifting* (Chosen), *A Divine Confrontation
... Birth Pangs of the New Church* (Destiny Image),
Crafted Prayer (Chosen) and *The Secret of a Powerful
Inner Life* (Chosen).

You can learn more about Graham Cooke at:

Graham Cooke
P.O. Box 91
Southampton
SO15 5ZE
United Kingdom

Website: www.grahamcooke.com